Prince Charming

poems by
Wolfgang Carstens

Prince Charming copyright © 2020 by Wolfgang Carstens. Art copyright © 2020 by Tracy Landers.

First edition. Printed in the USA.

Six Ft. Swells Press
www.sixftswellspress.com
www.facebook.com/SixFtSwells
Instagram: sixftswellspress

Editor: Todd Cirillo
www.toddcirillo.com

Graphic Design: Julie Valin
www.selftoshelfpublishing.com

Cover Photograph: Tracy Landers

Versions of some of these poems have previously appeared in *Bulletproof, From Dusk To Sandra Dawn, Perpetual Pallbearer, Love's An Infection, Trash and Ash, The Stench Of Failure, Three For The Road, Lummox,* Heroin Love Songs, Cajun Mutt Press, Rye Whiskey Review and The Smoking Typewriter.

Massive thanks, many cheers and monster love to my editor Todd Cirillo, a true friend—without whom many of these poems would never have happened.

All rights reserved. No part of this book may be reproduced in any manner without written permission except in the case of brief quotations included in critical essays, reviews and articles.

ISBN: 978-0-9853075-7-8

Contents

i sit alone 13
"have you ever 14
my publisher 16
forever 17
today, ... 18
"i need 19
the 20
"how old 21
i want my funeral 22
the first time 24
it was 26
what interests me 27
"i'm starting 28
my wife, ... 30
after too many beers, ... 31
the great irony 32
Beverly, ... 33
"hope 34
a perfect resume 36
when i ask 38
i shared 39
"you and i are soulmates," 40

when my wife 41
i woke up completely drunk 42
i used to believe 44
i have 46
on our first date, ... 48
i wake up 49
when my wife 50
i tried 51
i'm trapped 52
when Ray 54
"actually, ... 56
driving my wife 57
there's a guy 58
Sandra Dawn, ... 59
Dan 60
i just read 61
i wear shorts 62
in a drunken stupor, ... 64
i turned down 65

No Safe Spaces

Prince Charming is Wolfgang Carstens' extraordinary follow-up to the highly acclaimed *Hell And High Water* (Six Ft. Swells Press, 2017). This collection finds the poet expanding his shotgun eye towards everything he encounters, thinks of, considers, cares about or doesn't care for. There are no safe spaces in the poetry of Wolfgang Carstens. He writes without fear, taking on anything; poetry, philosophy, death itself and anyone; neighbors, strangers, children, ex-wives, even himself. His talent shines in presenting life as it is, not asking forgiveness or to change what is, such as in the opening poem, where neither the reader, nor the poet, can hide from the tragedy of loneliness. "i sit alone/ in front of my dying fire/ smoking cigarettes/ drinking beer…summer's gone/ and night/ is coming on/ hard."

These are poems of everyday moments and emotions; the pain of dear friends dying, the joy of being paid for poetry readings, the true love, playfulness and possible mistaken ménage à trois with his wife of 27 years, the hilarity and sharp humor of his children, shopping for groceries, living in a "gray and dismal" city, and the purity of friendship.

This is honest writing. Rarely can one find a more raw, heartbreakingly human moment than in his poem *How Old,* where the poet answers a question from his daughter. "how old/ was Aunt Beverly/ when she died?" The answer is a life altering moment of grave recognition between father and daughter, "she was/ as old as i am/ now/ i say/ we both/ fall silent".

Ultimately, beyond the brawling and bombastic humor in many of the poems, this book is about connection and confrontation. Connection of the poet to his children, his wife, his loves, his friends, his art and his worldview. Confrontation with death, aging, bad poetry, shit jobs, and those who don't understand the Warren Zevon philosophy. Carstens has the guts to put it all out there unapologetically. There is nowhere to run, nowhere to hide, no safe spaces. The reader and poetry itself deserve that much.

—Todd Cirillo, poet, editor
10:03 p.m. 3/3/20

For Tracy Lee

Prince Charming

poems by
Wolfgang Carstens

i sit alone

in front
of my dying fire,

smoking cigarettes,

drinking beer,

listening
to yellow
leaves

drop
from the trees.

summer's gone

and night

is
coming
on

hard.

"have you ever

been seriously hurt,"
she asked.

i boasted
about all

the motorbike crashes,
car crashes,

falling from buildings,
snowmobiles,
bicycles,
skateboards,
toboggans
and skis;

being attacked
by wild animals,
getting beat up,
robbed,
stabbed
and shot;

and how
despite
all of it,

i've never
been seriously
injured.

"well,"
she said,

"i guess
you'll be fine then,"

as she
picked up her bags
and walked
out.

my publisher

is paying me

$200 USD
to read poetry
for 20 minutes
in New Orleans.

i did the math.

that's almost $14
a minute Canadian.

funny,

my wife would pay
twice that

for me

to keep
my mouth
shut.

forever

the optimist,

for
her 90th
birthday,

she asked

for
a
clock.

today,

i texted my wife
to let her know
i was bringing
home some milk

but
autocorrect
changed it
to milf.

i discovered
the error
when she messaged me back
asking if the milf
was hot
and should she
send the kids
to the neighbors
for the night.

see,
that's why i love her.

it's also
the main reason
our marriage
has lasted 26 years.

she's always
willing to try
something

new.

"i need

to put my grades
up for adoption,"

Raven says.

"why is that,
Sweetheart,"

i ask,
laughing.

"because,"
she says,

"i just don't think
i can raise them

by myself."

the

saddest
part
of the poetry
slam
wasn't
that poetry
had been
reduced
to a
competition

but rather
it was
the runner up

sulking
in the
corner

still ranting
about
the
injustice
of it
all.

"how old

was Aunt Beverly
when she died,"

my daughter, Alexandria
asks.

"she was
as old as i am
now,"

i say.

we both
fall silent

and watch

the sun
slowly disappear

beneath
the ridge line.

i want my funeral

to be a party.

no dressing in black;
no veils;
no boo-fucking-hoo.

i want music,
dancing,
booze,
balloons,
and drugs.

put a bottle opener
on my casket;
pack it with ice
and turn it
into a beer cooler;

peel back my flesh
and turn my skull
into a hash bong.

just party motherfuckers!

celebrate the fact
that i'm dead
and you're not.

my ex-wives
have already RSVP'd.
they're picking out
new dresses
as we speak.

you should too.

and,
if you die first,

i promise

to do the
same.

the first time

i met Carol,
Ben's fiancé,

there was a bunch
of us gathered at his house
playing poker.

Carol came storming
from the bedroom
yelling at the top of her lungs:

"sure, you have time to play
goddamn poker
while the grass wasn't mowed,
hedges weren't trimmed,
fence wasn't repaired,
garbage wasn't out,
dishes aren't done,
bathroom's a mess,
bills are past due,"
on and on,
louder and louder.

it was a truly epic rant.

when she was finished,
i turned to Ben and said
"so,
when's the wedding?"

everyone burst into laughter,

except Ben,

whose face had turned
white as a sheet
as he quietly
folded
his cards.

it was

quite literally

the coldest place
on the planet

when my friend
mentioned
he wanted to visit.

"you wouldn't
like it here,"
i said.

"Edmonton's cold,
gray,
and dismal.

there's
nothing here."

to which he responded,
"you're there,
my friend."

and suddenly

it
didn't seem
like such a cold place

to be
after all.

what interests me

about
brilliant minds

is not so
much

who they
were,

or

what they
did,

but rather,

who
they chose

to spend
their lives

with.

"i'm starting

to look my age,"
my wife says,
as she's putting on
her makeup.

"no you're not,"
i say,
kissing her on the cheek.

"yes,"
she says,
"i look 40."

"well,"
i say,

"i guess i need
to trade you in
for a younger model."

"Honey,
i love you,"
she says,

"but there's
no other woman
on the face of the planet
that would put up
with your shit."

"that's not true,"
i say,
laughing,

"i'm charming."

"Prince of Darkness,
maybe,"
she says,

"but Prince Charming,
you're not."

"that's pretty good,"
i say,

"i'm gonna put that
in a poem."

"and that's another thing,"
she says,

"without me,
who's gonna write
your books

for you?"

my wife,

recently diagnosed
with rheumatoid arthritis,

started smoking pot
as a painkiller.

it's been strange
living with my stoned wife.

this morning, for example,
she was going on and on
about how we are born
from nothingness,
exist in nothingness,
and ultimately how
we return to nothingness.

"Jesus Honey," i said,
pouring my first cup of coffee,

"it's five thirty
in the morning,

i'm hungover as fuck,

i have to be at work
in less than an hour,

and if this is your idea
of a pep talk,

it's not fucking
working."

after too many beers,

i found myself
at a tattoo parlor.

"put my wife's name
right here,"
i said,

slapping
my right forearm.

stumbling
through the door
the next morning,

my wife
tore into me:

"where
have you been
all night,

who
were you with,

and
why the fuck
is BITCH
tattooed

on your arm?"

the great irony

is
that if
he hadn't
have been
born

with such
a small
penis

he
probably wouldn't
have been

such a
dick.

Beverly,

i saw
a little girl
who looked just
like you.

she
had your
smile.

it
had me thinking

Death
doesn't always

win.

"hope

is the greatest
evil,"
i said,

as i unbuttoned
her bra.

"that's ridiculous,"
she said.

"no, seriously,"
i said,
as i pulled
her pants down.

"hope keeps you
in a perpetual state
of suspense.

if you knew
the outcome—
good or bad,
you could plan
your life accordingly—

but no,
not with hope
dangling in front of you
like some proverbial jackpot.

there's a reason
why hope
was in Pandora's box,"

i said,
climbing under the sheets.

"well,"
she said,

"i hope
your brought a condom."

"damn,"
i said.

"i see what you mean,"
she laughed,
as she put her pants
back on.

"hope

can be
a cruel

bitch."

a perfect resume

landed on my desk.

his name was Barry.

his resume
was expertly worded,

highlighting
all the necessary skills,
qualifications,
and experience

any employer
could want
or wish for.

you'd be crazy
not to hire him.

instead of calling him in
for an interview,
i plagiarized his resume
and submitted it
to all the top companies.

i am presently employed
for $100,000 a year,
drive a company vehicle,
and enjoy
5 paid weeks of vacation
every year.

thanks Barry.

you are
the best employee
i never
hired.

when i ask

how
you are
doing,

you
say you
are living
the dream.

poor soul.

i
bet you
don't even

remember

falling
asleep.

i shared

the Bukowski quote,
"Find something you love
and let it kill you,"
with my wife.

"i found you, Mama,"
i said,
kissing her
on the forehead.

"first one
to the fetal position wins."

my wife just laughed,
blew me a kiss,
then said,

"game on,
motherfucker."

"you and i are soulmates,"

my wife said.

"i found you
in this world

and
i will find you
in the next,

and the next,
and the next.

i will never stop looking.
i will always find you."

"there you go,"
i said,

"again
with the

threats."

when my wife

began
rapidly losing
weight,

her friends
became worried
but never thought
it was exercise,
diet or discipline.
they were convinced
she was bulimic.

"no,"
i said,
putting the rumors
to rest.

"Tracy
hates throwing up.

also,
she doesn't like
putting things
down her throat.

trust me,

we've tried."

i woke up completely drunk.

i should've been at work
two hours ago
but have yet to leave
the house.

at any rate,
i began my day
by revisiting my reading
in Lawrence, Kansas.

i never realized
that i completely interrupted
the event organizer and host.

she's
literally in the middle
of introducing me
when i start my set.

yeah,
that's how
you pull the crowd on your side.

first, cut off the event organizer and host,
then read poems about fat women,
women who can't cook,
women who stalk you,
women whose genitals resemble mongooses,
women who don't give blowjobs,
about moving to Salt Lake City
with your sister wives,

then for good measure,
throw in a bunch of dick jokes—

all the while
being so drunk
you can barely speak.

well played Wolfgang,
you are a consummate
professional.

i used to believe

i was bullet-proof,

that if i just put blood
above my doorway,
Death would pass
me by.

i have never
broken a bone,
taken a ride
in an ambulance,
or spent a single night
in a hospital room.

i used to be the guy
when everyone around me
was dropping like flies,
who wouldn't get sick.

those days are gone.

now,
a simple cold
can leave me bedridden,

a flu,
like the one i have now,
can last for weeks,
sometimes months,

working its way
deep into my lungs.

today
marks my 45th year

and i am no longer
made of Kevlar.

the day is coming
when i will get sick
and not get any better.

happy birthday motherfucker!

your days
are
numbered.

i have

all these single
female friends—

and they
are always in need
of something—

computer repair,
changing a battery,
installing a thermostat,
etc—

so i start thinking
about moving
to Salt Lake City
with my Sister Wives—

but then look
at my wife
and quickly come
to my senses.

she
would never
go for it.

besides,
i can barely satisfy
her.

taking on
any more

would just be pressing
my luck.

on our first date,

she
let me
put my hand
down
her pants

and bring her
to full orgasm
in the movie
theater.

i
should've known

anything
that easy

would surely
go to

hell.

i wake up

drunk,

check for my wallet,
my phone,
my keys,

then light a cigarette
and try to remember

who i kissed,
who i danced with,
who i tried to fuck,
who i told
to fuck off,

and how the hell
i got here.

when my wife

was diagnosed
with anemia,

i researched
her condition
online.

"did you know
that when
your iron levels
are super low,
you can take
a piece of gold,
run it along the skin,
and it will leave
a black line—

we should try it,"
i said.

at this point,
my wife just laughed,
then said,

"Honey,
i'm married to you,

i don't have
any gold."

i tried

to divorce
my wife

by drinking her
to Death.

twenty-seven years
later,

it's anybody's
guess

who
will cross
the finish line

first.

i'm trapped

in a sexless marriage
with a woman
who is decomposing
before my eyes.

i wake up early,
make the kids lunch,
drop them off at school,
then go to a job i hate
to make ends meet.

i come home,
make supper,
listen to my wife complain,
my kids argue,
my dog bark,

then go upstairs
to my sexless bed,
climb between the sexless sheets
and have sexless dreams.

i am dying.

some say artists must suffer
for their craft.

Baby,
i've
suffered more
than most—

i may never
be well
again.

when Ray

was diagnosed
with stomach Cancer,

he went
from 100 pounds
overweight

to weighing
a mere 98
pounds.

when his friends
and family
talk about Ray,

they talk about how
Cancer ravaged him,

about how quickly
it devoured him,

and how
in the end
it didn't seem
like Ray at all.

when i talk
about Ray,

i talk about the times
he helped me shovel
my truck from the snowbank,

how we drank those beers
that time
when he showed me
the owls in his garage,

and how he was one
of the nicest
kindest,
most generous
individuals
i ever knew.

when i talk about Ray,

i never
talk about
Cancer.

"actually,

they say
the skin
is the largest organ
in the human
body."

"well,"
she said,
licking her lips,

"meet me
upstairs
in fifteen minutes

and
let me
be
the judge

of
that."

driving my wife

to work,
she was on
a rant
from hell:

dishes,
laundry,
yard work.

as
we dropped
her off,

i turned
to my daughter
and said

"yeah,
that's your mother."

"true,"
she said,

"but

at least
i wasn't the dumb
bastard

who married
her."

there's a guy

standing outside the liquor store
with a cardboard sign
that reads:

BROKE AND HUNGRY.
EVERY LITTLE BIT HELPS.

"excuse me, Sir."
i say,
as i put a five dollar bill into his hand,

"you spelled THIRSTY
wrong."

Sandra Dawn,

thank you
for the one cent
child support payment
this month.

it will
come in handy
if our son and i
come across

any
train tracks.

Dan

loved irony.

he
had been
working out
eight months

and went
from 197 pounds
to a lean 171.

at 43,
he was in
the best shape
of his life.

that's
when the heart attack
took him.

Dan
would've fucking
loved

that.

i just read

quite possibly
the worst poem
ever written
in the English
language.

it may
have been
yours.

i wear shorts

every day,

all year,

whether
it's plus 30
or minus 40.

lots of people
in Alberta
rarely go outside
in winter.

for me,
it's like Zevon's sandwich,
every day
above blades of grass
is a good day.

they say
i'm crazy.

i
say they don't
understand

the Warren Zevon
philosophy.

most only ask
"who is Warren Zevon?"

i tell them
it's getting cold out here,
probably time for them
to head back indoors.

in a drunken stupor,

clawing my way
across the floor
on my hands and knees
like a wounded animal,

i started thinking
about great exit lines—

something
worthy of a tombstone.

ultimately,
all i could come up with
was:

surely,
one more
won't kill
me.

i turned down

a job
for $85,000
a year

because
it required me
to travel

fourteen days
every month.

i don't want
to be
without my wife
for one day,

let alone
six months
every year.

$85,000.

and to think
my wife
complains

that i don't
write

love poems.

Wolfgang Carstens lives in Canada with his wife, five kids, grandson, two cats, the memory of a good dog, mortgage and death. His poetry is printed on the backs of unpaid bills. More information at wolfgangcarstens.com.

www.ingramcontent.com/pod-product-compliance
Lightning Source LLC
Chambersburg PA
CBHW060427050426
42449CB00009B/2176